GREEK

ENGLISH

dictionary

ΜΉΛΟ

mílo

apple

ΦΡΆΟΥΛΑ

fráoula

strawberry

ΣΚΎΛΟΣ

skýlos

dog

ГАТА

gáta

cat

ΣΠΙΤΙ

spíti

house

ΚλΕΙΔΙΑ

kleidiá

keys

NTOMÁTA

ntomáta

tomato

KAPOTO

karóto

carrot

Ήλιος

ílios

sun

ΟΥΡΑΝΙΟ ΤΟΞΟ

ouránio tóxo

rainbow

ΚΥΚΛΟΣ

kýklos

circle

TPIΓΟΝΟ

trigono

triangle

ΦΥΤΟ

fytó

plant

ΤΡΑΠΕΖΙ

trapézi

table

ΛΟΥΛΟΎΔΙ

louloúdi

flower

ΣΑΛΙΓΚΆΡΙ

salinkári

snail

AYTOKINHTO

aftokinito

car

TPENO

tréno

train

ΦΛΙΤΖΆΝΙ

flitzáni

cup

ΚΟΥΤΑΛΙ

koutáli

spoon

ΠΑΓΩΤΟ

pagotó

ice cream

K'EIK

kéik

cake

ΚΆΛΤΣΕΣ

kάltses

socks

ΚΟΝΤΟΜΆΝΙΚΗ ΜΠΛΟΎΖΑ

kontomániki bloúza

T-shirt

ВРОХН

vrochi

rain

OMΠΡΈΛΑ

ompréla

umbrella

ΔΈΝΤΡΟ

déntro

tree

ΠΕΤΑΛΟΎΔΑ

petaloúda

butterfly

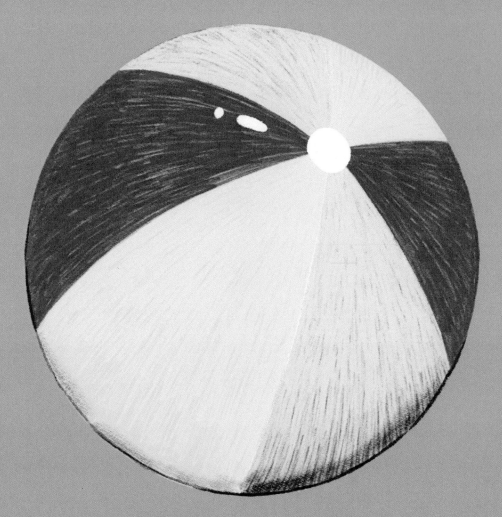

ΜΠΆΛΑ

bála

ball

ΚΆΔΟΣ

kádos

bucket

ΔΏΡΟ

dóro

gift

ΑΡΚΟΥΔΆΚΙ

arkoudáki

teddy bear

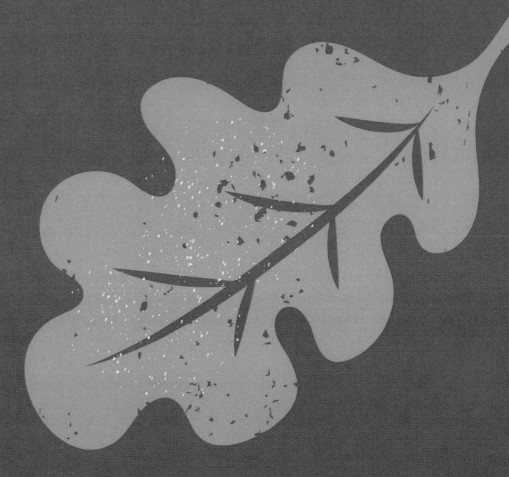

ΦΥΛΛΟ

fÿllo

leaf

MANITAPI

manitári

mushroom

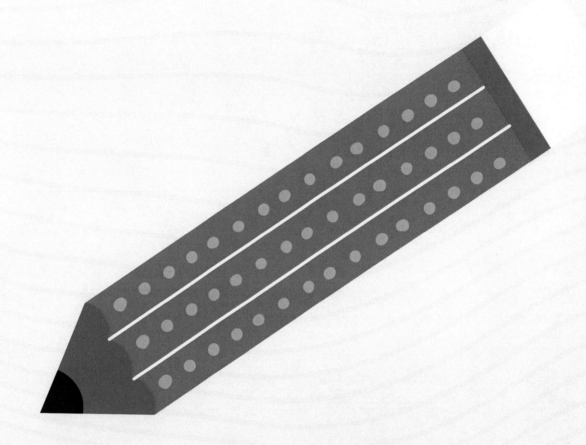

ΜΟΛΎΒΙ

molývi

pencil

BIBΛΊO

viulío

book

ΦOPEMA

fórema

dress

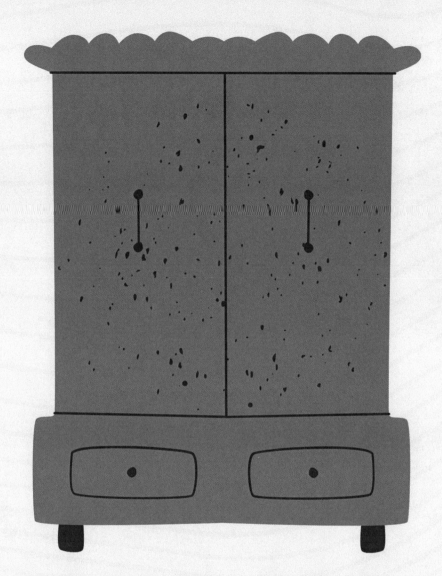

ΝΤΟΥΛΆΠΑ

ntoulápa

wardrobe

ΝΑΙ

yes

ΌΧΙ

no

ΚΑΛΗΜΈΡΑ

good morning

ΕΥΧΑΡΙΣΤΏ

thanks

Made in United States
Orlando, FL
30 November 2024

54649204R00024